Action Plan on Base Erosion and Profit Shifting

This work is published on the responsibility of the Secretary-General of the OECD. The opinions expressed and arguments employed herein do not necessarily reflect the official views of the Organisation or of the governments of its member countries.

This document and any map included herein are without prejudice to the status of or sovereignty over any territory, to the delimitation of international frontiers and boundaries and to the name of any territory, city or area.

Please cite this publication as:
OECD (2013), *Action Plan on Base Erosion and Profit Shifting*, OECD Publishing.
http://dx.doi.org/10.1787/9789264202719-en

ISBN 978-92-64-20270-2 (print)
ISBN 978-92-64-20271-9 (PDF)

Photo credits: Cover © iStockphoto.com/apsimo1, © iStockphoto.com/Silvrshootr, © Oleksiy Mark / Shuttestock.com.

Corrigenda to OECD publications may be found on line at: *www.oecd.org/publishing/corrigenda*.
© OECD 2013

You can copy, download or print OECD content for your own use, and you can include excerpts from OECD publications, databases and multimedia products in your own documents, presentations, blogs, websites and teaching materials, provided that suitable acknowledgment of the source and copyright owner is given. All requests for public or commercial use and translation rights should be submitted to *rights@oecd.org*. Requests for permission to photocopy portions of this material for public or commercial use shall be addressed directly to the Copyright Clearance Center (CCC) at *info@copyright.com* or the Centre français d'exploitation du droit de copie (CFC) at *contact@cfcopies.com*.

Table of contents

Acronyms and abbreviations 5

Chapter 1. **Introduction** 7

Chapter 2. **Background** 9

Chapter 3. **Action Plan** 13

    A. Actions 14
        (i) Establishing international coherence of corporate income taxation 15
        (ii) Restoring the full effects and benefits of international standards 18
        (iii) Ensuring transparency while promoting increased certainty and predictability 21
        (iv) From agreed policies to tax rules: the need for a swift implementation of the measures 23

    B. Timing 24

    C. Methodology 25
        (i) An inclusive and effective process: launching the OECD/G20 BEPS Project and involving developing countries 25
        (ii) Efficient process 26
        (iii) Consulting with business and civil society 26

References 27

Annex A. **Overview of the actions and timelines** 29

Tables

Table A.1   Summary of the BEPS Action Plan by action 29
Table A.2   Summary of the BEPS Action Plan by timeline 35

Acronyms and abbreviations

BEPS	Base erosion and profit shifting
BIAC	Business and Industry Advisory Committee to the OECD
CFA	Committee on Fiscal Affairs
CFC	Controlled foreign company
FDI	Foreign direct investment
FHTP	Forum on Harmful Tax Practices
GDP	Gross domestic product
MAP	Mutual agreement procedure
MNE	Multinational enterprise
OECD	Organisation for Economic Co-operation and Development
PE	Permanent establishment
TFTD	Task Force on Tax and Development
TUAC	Trade Union Advisory Committee to the OECD
UN	United Nations
VAT	Value added tax
VAT/GST	Value added tax/Goods and services tax

Chapter 1

Introduction

Globalisation has benefited our domestic economies. Globalisation is not new, but the pace of integration of national economies and markets has increased substantially in recent years. The free movement of capital and labour, the shift of manufacturing bases from high-cost to low-cost locations, the gradual removal of trade barriers, technological and telecommunication developments, and the ever-increasing importance of managing risks and of developing, protecting and exploiting intellectual property, have had an important impact on the way cross-border activities take place. Globalisation has boosted trade and increased foreign direct investments in many countries. Hence it supports growth, creates jobs, fosters innovation, and has lifted millions out of poverty.

Globalisation impacts countries' corporate income tax regimes. As long ago as the 1920s, the League of Nations recognised that the interaction of domestic tax systems can lead to double taxation with adverse effects on growth and global prosperity. Countries around the world agree on the need to eliminate double taxation and the need to achieve this on the basis of agreed international rules that are clear and predictable, giving certainty to both governments and businesses. International tax law is therefore a key pillar in supporting the growth of the global economy.

As the economy became more globally integrated, so did corporations. Multi-national enterprises (MNE) now represent a large proportion of global GDP. Also, intra-firm trade represents a growing proportion of overall trade. Globalisation has resulted in a shift from country-specific operating models to global models based on matrix management organisations and integrated supply chains that centralise several functions at a regional or global level. Moreover, the growing importance of the service component of the economy, and of digital products that often can be delivered over the Internet, has made it much easier for businesses to locate many productive activities in geographic locations that are distant from the physical location of their customers. These developments have been exacerbated by the increasing sophistication of tax planners in identifying and exploiting the legal arbitrage opportunities and the boundaries of acceptable tax planning, thus providing MNEs with more confidence in taking aggressive tax positions.

These developments have opened up opportunities for MNEs to greatly minimise their tax burden. This has led to a tense situation in which citizens have become more sensitive to tax fairness issues. It has become a critical issue for all parties:

- *Governments are harmed.* Many governments have to cope with less revenue and a higher cost to ensure compliance. Moreover, Base Erosion and Profit Shifting (BEPS) undermines the integrity of the tax system, as the public, the media and some taxpayers deem reported low corporate taxes to be unfair. In developing countries, the lack of tax revenue leads to critical under-funding of public investment that could help promote economic growth. Overall resource allocation, affected by tax-motivated behaviour, is not optimal.

- *Individual taxpayers are harmed.* When tax rules permit businesses to reduce their tax burden by shifting their income away from jurisdictions where income producing activities are conducted, other taxpayers in that jurisdiction bear a greater share of the burden.

- *Businesses are harmed.* MNEs may face significant reputational risk if their effective tax rate is viewed as being too low. At the same time, different businesses may assess such risk differently, and failing to take advantage of legal opportunities to reduce an enterprise's tax burden can put it at a competitive disadvantage. Similarly, corporations that operate only in domestic markets, including family-owned businesses or new innovative companies, have difficulty competing with MNEs that have the ability to shift their profits across borders to avoid or reduce tax. Fair competition is harmed by the distortions induced by BEPS.

Chapter 2

Background

Taxation is at the core of countries' sovereignty, but the interaction of domestic tax rules in some cases leads to gaps and frictions. When designing their domestic tax rules, sovereign states may not sufficiently take into account the effect of other countries' rules. The interaction of independent sets of rules enforced by sovereign countries creates frictions, including potential double taxation for corporations operating in several countries. It also creates gaps, in cases where corporate income is not taxed at all, either by the country of source or the country of residence, or is only taxed at nominal rates. In the domestic context, coherence is usually achieved through a principle of matching – a payment that is deductible by the payer is generally taxable in the hands of the recipient, unless explicitly exempted. There is no similar principle of coherence at the international level, which leaves plenty of room for arbitrage by taxpayers, though sovereign states have co-operated to ensure coherence in a narrow field, namely to prevent double taxation.

The international standards have sought to address these frictions in a way that respects tax sovereignty, but gaps remain. Since at least the 1920s, it has been recognised that the interaction of domestic tax systems can lead to overlaps in the exercise of taxing rights that in turn can result in double taxation. Countries have long worked and are strongly committed to eliminate such double taxation in order to minimise trade distortions and impediments to sustainable economic growth, while affirming their sovereign right to establish their own tax rules. There are gaps and frictions among different countries' tax systems that were not taken in account in designing the existing standards and which are not dealt with by bilateral tax treaties. The global economy requires countries to collaborate on tax matters in order to be able to protect their tax sovereignty.

In many circumstances, the existing domestic law and treaty rules governing the taxation of cross-border profits produce the correct results and do not give rise to BEPS. International co-operation has resulted in shared principles and a network of thousands of bilateral tax treaties that are based on common standards and that therefore generally result in the prevention of double taxation on profits from cross-border activities. Clarity and predictability are fundamental building blocks of economic growth. It is important to retain such clarity and predictability by building on this experience. At the same time, instances where the current rules give rise to results that generate concerns from a policy perspective should be tackled.

Over time, the current rules have also revealed weaknesses that create opportunities for BEPS. BEPS relates chiefly to instances where the interaction of different tax rules leads to double non-taxation or less than single taxation. It also relates to arrangements that achieve no or low taxation by shifting profits away from the jurisdictions where the activities creating those profits take place. No or low taxation is not *per se* a cause of concern, but it becomes so when it is associated with practices that artificially segregate taxable income from the activities that generate it. In other words, what creates tax policy concerns is that, due to gaps in the interaction of different tax systems, and in some cases because of the application of bilateral tax treaties, income from cross-border activities may go untaxed anywhere, or be only unduly lowly taxed.

The spread of the digital economy also poses challenges for international taxation. The digital economy is characterised by an unparalleled reliance on intangible assets, the massive use of data (notably personal data), the widespread adoption of multi-sided business models capturing value from externalities generated by free products, and the difficulty of determining the jurisdiction in which value creation occurs. This raises fundamental questions as to how enterprises in the digital economy add value and make their profits, and how the digital economy relates to the concepts of source and residence or the characterisation of income for tax purposes. At the same time, the fact that new ways of doing business may result in a relocation of core business functions and, consequently, a different distribution of taxing rights which may lead to low taxation is not *per se* an indicator of defects in the existing system. It is important to examine closely how enterprises of the digital economy add value and make their profits in order to determine whether and to what extent it may be necessary to adapt the current rules in order to take into account the specific features of that industry and to prevent BEPS.

These weaknesses put the existing consensus-based framework at risk, and a bold move by policy makers is necessary to prevent worsening problems. Inaction in this area would likely result in some governments losing corporate tax revenue, the emergence of competing sets of international standards, and the replacement of the current consensus-based framework by unilateral measures, which could lead to global tax chaos marked by the massive re-emergence of double taxation. In fact, if the Action Plan fails to develop effective solutions in a timely manner, some countries may be persuaded to take unilateral action for protecting their tax base, resulting in avoidable uncertainty and unrelieved double taxation. It is therefore critical that governments achieve consensus on actions that would deal with the above weaknesses. As the G20 Leaders pointed out, "Despite the challenges we all face domestically, we have agreed that multilateralism is of even greater importance in the current climate, and remains our best asset to resolve the global economy's difficulties" (G20, 2012).

In the changing international tax environment, a number of countries have expressed a concern about how international standards on which bilateral tax treaties are based allocate taxing rights between source and residence States. This Action Plan is focused on addressing BEPS. While actions to address BEPS will restore both source and residence taxation in a number of cases where cross-border income would otherwise go untaxed or would be taxed at very low rates, these actions are not directly aimed at changing the existing international standards on the allocation of taxing rights on cross-border income.

The G20 finance ministers called on the OECD to develop an action plan to address BEPS issues in a co-ordinated and comprehensive manner. Specifically, this Action Plan should provide countries with domestic and international instruments that will better align rights to tax with economic activity. As called for in the recent OECD report on BEPS, *Addressing Base Erosion and Profit Shifting* (OECD, 2013a), this Action Plan *(i)* identifies actions needed to address BEPS, *(ii)* sets deadlines to implement these actions and *(iii)* identifies the resources needed and the methodology to implement these actions.

Chapter 3

Action Plan

Fundamental changes are needed to effectively prevent double non-taxation, as well as cases of no or low taxation associated with practices that artificially segregate taxable income from the activities that generate it. A number of actions can be undertaken in order to address the weaknesses in the current rules in an effective and efficient manner. This Action Plan calls for fundamental changes to the current mechanisms and the adoption of new consensus-based approaches, including anti-abuse provisions, designed to prevent and counter base erosion and profit shifting:

New International standards must be designed to ensure the coherence of corporate income taxation at the international level. BEPS issues may arise directly from the existence of loopholes, as well as gaps, frictions or mismatches in the interaction of countries' domestic tax laws. These types of issues generally have not been dealt with by OECD standards or bilateral treaty provisions. There is a need to complement existing standards that are designed to prevent double taxation with instruments that prevent double non-taxation in areas previously not covered by international standards and that address cases of no or low taxation associated with practices that artificially segregate taxable income from the activities that generate it. Moreover, governments must continue to work together to tackle harmful tax practices and aggressive tax planning.

A realignment of taxation and relevant substance is needed to restore the intended effects and benefits of international standards, which may not have kept pace with changing business models and technological developments:

- Whilst bilateral tax treaties have been effective in preventing double taxation, there is a concern that they often fail to prevent double non-taxation that results from interactions among more than two countries. In particular, the involvement of third countries in the bilateral framework established by treaty partners puts a strain on the existing rules, in particular when done via shell companies that have little or no substance in terms of office space, tangible assets and employees.

- In the area of transfer pricing, the rules should be improved in order to put more emphasis on value creation in highly integrated groups, tackling the use of intangibles, risks, capital and other high-risk transactions to shift profits. At the same time, there is consensus among governments that moving to a system of formulary apportionment of profits is not a viable way forward; it is also unclear that the behavioural changes companies might adopt in response to the use of a formula would lead to investment decisions that are more efficient and tax-neutral than under a separate entity approach.

The actions implemented to counter BEPS cannot succeed without further transparency, nor without certainty and predictability for business. The availability of timely, targeted and comprehensive information is essential to enable governments to quickly identify risk areas. While audits remain a key source of relevant information, they suffer from a number of constraints and from a lack of relevant tools for the early detection of aggressive tax planning. As a result, timely, comprehensive and relevant information on tax planning strategies is often unavailable to tax administrations, and new mechanisms to obtain that information must be developed. At the same time, mechanisms should be implemented to provide businesses with the certainty and predictability they need to make investment decisions.

A. Actions

BEPS is a concern in the context of the digital economy. The actions will help address these concerns. However, there are specificities that need to be taken into consideration. This will require a thorough analysis of the different business models, the ever-changing business landscape and a better understanding of the generation of value in this sector. Moreover, indirect tax aspects should also be considered. Drawing on the other actions included in this plan, a dedicated task force on the digital economy will be established.

ACTION 1
Address the tax challenges of the digital economy

Identify the main difficulties that the digital economy poses for the application of existing international tax rules and develop detailed options to address these difficulties, taking a holistic approach and considering both direct and indirect taxation. Issues to be examined include, but are not limited to, the ability of a company to have a significant digital presence in the economy of another country without being liable to taxation due to the lack of nexus under current international rules, the attribution of value created from the generation of marketable location-relevant data through the use of digital products and services, the characterisation of income derived from new business models, the application of related source rules, and how to ensure the effective collection of VAT/GST with respect to the cross-border supply of digital goods and services. Such work will require a thorough analysis of the various business models in this sector.

(i) Establishing international coherence of corporate income taxation

Globalisation means that domestic policies, including tax policy, cannot be designed in isolation. Tax policy is at the core of countries' sovereignty, and each country has the right to design its tax system in the way it considers most appropriate. At the same time, the increasing interconnectedness of domestic economies has highlighted the gaps that can be created by interactions between domestic tax laws. Therefore, there is a need to complement rules to prevent double taxation with a fundamentally new set of standards designed to establish international coherence in corporate income taxation.

Four main issues have been identified:

The BEPS report (OECD, 2013a) calls for the development of "instruments to put an end to or neutralise the effects of hybrid mismatch arrangements and arbitrage". Hybrid mismatch arrangements can be used to achieve unintended double non-taxation or long-term tax deferral by, for instance, creating two deductions for one borrowing, generating deductions without corresponding income inclusions, or misusing foreign tax credit and participation exemption regimes. Country rules that allow taxpayers to choose the tax treatment of certain domestic and foreign entities could facilitate hybrid mismatches. While it may be difficult to determine which country has in fact lost tax revenue, because the laws of each country involved have been followed, there is a reduction of the overall tax paid by all parties involved as a whole, which harms competition, economic efficiency, transparency and fairness.

ACTION 2

Neutralise the effects of hybrid mismatch arrangements

Develop model treaty provisions and recommendations regarding the design of domestic rules to neutralise the effect (e.g. double non-taxation, double deduction, long-term deferral) of hybrid instruments and entities. This may include: (i) changes to the OECD Model Tax Convention to ensure that hybrid instruments and entities (as well as dual resident entities) are not used to obtain the benefits of treaties unduly; (ii) domestic law provisions that prevent exemption or non-recognition for payments that are deductible by the payor; (iii) domestic law provisions that deny a deduction for a payment that is not includible in income by the recipient (and is not subject to taxation under controlled foreign company (CFC) or similar rules); (iv) domestic law provisions that deny a deduction for a payment that is also deductible in another jurisdiction; and (v) where necessary, guidance on co-ordination or tie-breaker rules if more than one country seeks to apply such rules to a transaction or structure. Special attention should be given to the interaction between possible changes to domestic law and the provisions of the OECD Model Tax Convention. This work will be co-ordinated with the work on interest expense deduction limitations, the work on CFC rules, and the work on treaty shopping.

One area in which the OECD has not done significant work in the past is CFC rules. One of the sources of BEPS concerns is the possibility of creating affiliated non-resident taxpayers and routing income of a resident enterprise through the non-resident affiliate. CFC and other anti-deferral rules have been introduced in many countries to address this issue. However, the CFC rules of many countries do not always counter BEPS in a comprehensive manner. While CFC rules in principle lead to inclusions in the residence country of the ultimate parent, they also have positive spillover effects in *source countries* because taxpayers have no (or much less of an) incentive to shift profits into a third, low-tax jurisdiction.

ACTION 3
Strengthen CFC rules

Develop recommendations regarding the design of controlled foreign company rules. This work will be co-ordinated with other work as necessary.

Another issue raising BEPS concerns is excessive deductible payments such as interest and other financial payments. The deductibility of interest expense can give rise to double non-taxation in both the inbound and outbound investment scenarios. From an inbound perspective, the concern regarding interest expense deduction is primarily with lending from a related entity that benefits from a low-tax regime, to create excessive interest deductions for the issuer without a corresponding interest income inclusion by the holder. The result is that the interest payments are deducted against the taxable profits of the operating companies while the interest income is taxed favourably or not at all at the level of the recipient, and sometimes the group as a whole may have little or no external debt. From an outbound perspective, a company may use debt to finance the production of exempt or deferred income, thereby claiming a current deduction for interest expense while deferring or exempting the related income. Rules regarding the deductibility of interest expense therefore should take into account that the related interest income may not be fully taxed or that the underlying debt may be used to inappropriately reduce the earnings base of the issuer or finance deferred or exempt income. Related concerns are raised by deductible payments for other financial transactions, such as financial and performance guarantees, derivatives, and captive and other insurance arrangements, particularly in the context of transfer pricing.

ACTION 4
Limit base erosion via interest deductions and other financial payments

Develop recommendations regarding best practices in the design of rules to prevent base erosion through the use of interest expense, for example through the use of related-party and third-party debt to achieve excessive interest deductions or to finance the production of exempt or deferred income, and other financial payments that are economically equivalent to interest payments. The work will evaluate the effectiveness of different types of limitations. In connection with and in support of the foregoing work, transfer pricing guidance will also be developed regarding the pricing of related party financial transactions, including financial and performance guarantees, derivatives (including internal derivatives used in intra-bank dealings), and captive and other insurance arrangements. The work will be co-ordinated with the work on hybrids and CFC rules.

Preferential regimes continue to be a key pressure area. In 1998, the OECD issued a report (OECD, 1998) on harmful tax practices in part based on the recognition that a "race to the bottom" would ultimately drive applicable tax rates on certain mobile sources of income to zero for all countries, whether or not this was the tax policy a country wished to pursue. Agreeing to a set of common rules may in fact help countries to make their sovereign tax policy choices. The underlying policy concerns expressed in the 1998 Report as regards the "race to the bottom" on the mobile income tax base are as relevant today as they were 15 years ago. However, the "race to the bottom" nowadays often takes less the form of traditional ring-fencing and more the form of across the board corporate tax rate reductions on particular types of income (such as income from financial activities or from the provision of intangibles). The BEPS report (OECD, 2013a) calls for proposals to develop "solutions to counter harmful regimes more effectively, taking into account factors such as transparency and substance." In furtherance of this goal, the work of the Forum on Harmful Tax Practices (FHTP) will be refocused to develop more effective solutions.

ACTION 5
Counter harmful tax practices more effectively, taking into account transparency and substance

Revamp the work on harmful tax practices with a priority on improving transparency, including compulsory spontaneous exchange on rulings related to preferential regimes, and on requiring substantial activity for any preferential regime. It will take a holistic approach to evaluate preferential tax regimes in the BEPS context. It will engage with non-OECD members on the basis of the existing framework and consider revisions or additions to the existing framework.

(ii) Restoring the full effects and benefits of international standards

Current rules work well in many cases, but they need to be adapted to prevent BEPS that results from the interactions among more than two countries and to fully account for global value chains. The interposition of third countries in the bilateral framework established by treaty partners has led to the development of schemes such as low-taxed branches of a foreign company, conduit companies, and the artificial shifting of income through transfer pricing arrangements. FDI figures show the magnitude of the use of certain regimes to channel investments and intra-group financing from one country to another through conduit structures. In order to preserve the intended effects of bilateral relationships, the rules must be modified to address the use of multiple layers of legal entities inserted between the residence country and the source country.

Existing domestic and international tax rules should be modified in order to more closely align the allocation of income with the economic activity that generates that income:

Treaty abuse is one of the most important sources of BEPS concerns. The Commentary on Article 1 of the OECD Model Tax Convention already includes a number of examples of provisions that could be used to address treaty-shopping situations as well as other cases of treaty abuse, which may give rise to double non-taxation. Tight treaty anti-abuse clauses coupled with the exercise of taxing rights under domestic laws will contribute to restore source taxation in a number of cases.

ACTION 6
Prevent treaty abuse

Develop model treaty provisions and recommendations regarding the design of domestic rules to prevent the granting of treaty benefits in inappropriate circumstances. Work will also be done to clarify that tax treaties are not intended to be used to generate double non-taxation and to identify the tax policy considerations that, in general, countries should consider before deciding to enter into a tax treaty with another country. The work will be co-ordinated with the work on hybrids.

The definition of permanent establishment (PE) must be updated to prevent abuses. In many countries, the interpretation of the treaty rules on agency-PE allows contracts for the sale of goods belonging to a foreign enterprise to be negotiated and concluded in a country by the sales force of a local subsidiary of that foreign enterprise without the profits from these sales being taxable to the same extent as they would be if the sales were made by a distributor. In many cases, this has led enterprises to replace arrangements under which the local subsidiary traditionally acted as a distributor by "commissionnaire arrangements" with a resulting shift of profits out of the country where the sales take place without a substantive change in the functions performed in that country. Similarly, MNEs may artificially fragment their operations among multiple group entities to qualify for the exceptions to PE status for preparatory and ancillary activities.

ACTION 7
Prevent the artificial avoidance of PE status

Develop changes to the definition of PE to prevent the artificial avoidance of PE status in relation to BEPS, including through the use of commissionaire arrangements and the specific activity exemptions. Work on these issues will also address related profit attribution issues.

A major issue is transfer pricing and the enforcement of the arm's length principle. Transfer pricing rules serve to allocate income earned by a multinational enterprise among those countries in which the company does business. In many instances, the existing transfer pricing rules, based on the arm's length principle, effectively and efficiently allocate the income of multinationals among taxing jurisdictions. In other instances, however, multinationals have been able to use and/or misapply those rules to separate income from the economic activities that produce that income and to shift it into low-tax environments. This most often results from transfers of intangibles and other mobile assets for less than full value, the over-capitalisation of lowly taxed group companies and from contractual allocations of risk to low-tax environments in transactions that would be unlikely to occur between unrelated parties.

Alternative income allocation systems, including formula based systems, are sometimes suggested. However, the importance of concerted action and the practical difficulties associated with agreeing to and implementing the details of a new system consistently across all countries mean that, rather than seeking to replace the current transfer pricing system, the best course is to directly address the flaws in the current system, in particular with respect to returns related to intangible assets, risk and over-capitalisation. Nevertheless, special measures, either within or beyond the arm's length principle, may be required with respect to intangible assets, risk and over-capitalisation to address these flaws.

ACTIONS 8, 9, 10
Assure that transfer pricing outcomes are in line with value creation

Action 8 – Intangibles

Develop rules to prevent BEPS by moving intangibles among group members. This will involve: (i) adopting a broad and clearly delineated definition of intangibles; (ii) ensuring that profits associated with the transfer and use of intangibles are appropriately allocated in accordance with (rather than divorced from) value creation; (iii) developing transfer pricing rules or special measures for transfers of hard-to-value intangibles; and (iv) updating the guidance on cost contribution arrangements.

Action 9 – Risks and capital

Develop rules to prevent BEPS by transferring risks among, or allocating excessive capital to, group members. This will involve adopting transfer pricing rules or special measures to ensure that inappropriate returns will not accrue to an entity solely because it has contractually assumed risks or has provided capital. The rules to be developed will also require alignment of returns with value creation. This work will be co-ordinated with the work on interest expense deductions and other financial payments.

Action 10 – Other high-risk transactions

Develop rules to prevent BEPS by engaging in transactions which would not, or would only very rarely, occur between third parties. This will involve adopting transfer pricing rules or special measures to: (i) clarify the circumstances in which transactions can be recharacterised; (ii) clarify the application of transfer pricing methods, in particular profit splits, in the context of global value chains; and (iii) provide protection against common types of base eroding payments, such as management fees and head office expenses.

(iii) Ensuring transparency while promoting increased certainty and predictability

Preventing BEPS implies transparency at different levels. Progress on transparency has been made by the Global Forum on Transparency and Exchange of Information for Tax Purposes, but the need for a more holistic approach has been revealed when it comes to preventing BEPS, which implies more transparency on different fronts. Data collection on BEPS should be improved. Taxpayers should disclose more targeted information about their tax planning strategies, and transfer pricing documentation requirements should be less burdensome and more targeted.

Improving the availability and analysis of data on BEPS is critical, including to monitor the implementation of the Action Plan. The BEPS report (OECD, 2013a) notes that there are several studies and data indicating that there is an increased disconnect between the location where value creating activities and investment take place and the location where profits are reported for tax purposes. The report noted that further work needs to be done to evaluate such studies, to develop measures of the scale and effects of BEPS behaviours, and to monitor the impact of measures taken under the Action Plan to address BEPS. This should include outcome-based techniques, which look at measures of the allocation of income across jurisdictions relative to measures of value creating activities, as well as techniques that can be used to monitor the specific issues identified in the Action Plan. Accordingly, it is important to identify the types of data that taxpayers should provide to tax administrators, as well as the methodologies that can be used to analyse these data and to assess the likely economic implications of BEPS behaviours and actions taken to address BEPS.

ACTION 11
Establish methodologies to collect and analyse data on BEPS and the actions to address it

Develop recommendations regarding indicators of the scale and economic impact of BEPS and ensure that tools are available to monitor and evaluate the effectiveness and economic impact of the actions taken to address BEPS on an ongoing basis. This will involve developing an economic analysis of the scale and impact of BEPS (including spillover effects across countries) and actions to address it. *The work will also involve assessing a range of existing data sources, identifying new types of data that should be collected, and developing methodologies based on both aggregate (e.g. FDI and balance of payments data) and micro-level data (e.g. from financial statements and tax returns), taking into consideration the need to respect taxpayer confidentiality and the administrative costs for tax administrations and businesses.*

Transparency on certain tax planning/transactions is also needed. Comprehensive and relevant information on tax planning strategies is often unavailable to tax administrations. Yet the availability of timely, targeted and comprehensive information is essential to enable governments to quickly identify risk areas. While audits remain a key source of relevant information, they suffer from a number of constraints as tools for the early detection of aggressive tax planning techniques. Measures designed to improve information flow about tax risks to tax administrations and tax policy makers ("disclosure initiatives") may be useful in this regard. Other potentially useful measures include co-operative compliance programmes between taxpayers and tax administrations (see OECD, 2013b).

ACTION 12
Require taxpayers to disclose their aggressive tax planning arrangements

Develop recommendations regarding the design of mandatory disclosure rules for aggressive or abusive transactions, arrangements, or structures, taking into consideration the administrative costs for tax administrations and businesses and drawing on experiences of the increasing number of countries that have such rules. The work will use a modular design allowing for maximum consistency but allowing for country specific needs and risks. One focus will be international tax schemes, where the work will explore using a wide definition of "tax benefit" in order to capture such transactions. The work will be co-ordinated with the work on co-operative compliance. It will also involve designing and putting in place enhanced models of information sharing for international tax schemes between tax administrations.

Transparency also relates to transfer pricing and value-chain analyses. A key issue in the administration of transfer pricing rules is the asymmetry of information between taxpayers and tax administrations. This potentially undermines the administration of the arm's length principle and enhances opportunities for BEPS. In many countries, tax administrations have little capability of developing a "big picture" view of a taxpayer's global value chain. In addition, divergences between approaches to transfer pricing documentation requirements leads to significant administrative costs for businesses. In this respect, it is important that adequate information about the relevant functions performed by other members of the MNE group in respect of intra-group services and other transactions is made available to the tax administration.

ACTION 13
Re-examine transfer pricing documentation

Develop rules regarding transfer pricing documentation to enhance transparency for tax administration, taking into consideration the compliance costs for business. The rules to be developed will include a requirement that MNE's provide all relevant governments with needed information on their global allocation of the income, economic activity and taxes paid among countries according to a common template.

The actions to counter BEPS must be complemented with actions that ensure certainty and predictability for business. Work to improve the effectiveness of the mutual agreement procedure (MAP) will be an important complement to the work on BEPS issues. The interpretation and application of novel rules resulting from the work described above could introduce elements of uncertainty that should be minimised as much as possible. Work will therefore be undertaken in order to examine and address obstacles that prevent countries from solving treaty-related disputes under the MAP. Consideration will also be given to supplementing the existing MAP provisions in tax treaties with a mandatory and binding arbitration provision.

ACTION 14
Make dispute resolution mechanisms more effective

Develop solutions to address obstacles that prevent countries from solving treaty-related disputes under MAP, including the absence of arbitration provisions in most treaties and the fact that access to MAP and arbitration may be denied in certain cases.

(iv) From agreed policies to tax rules: the need for a swift implementation of the measures

There is a need to consider innovative ways to implement the measures resulting from the work on the BEPS Action Plan. The delivery of the actions included in the Action Plan on BEPS will result in a number of outputs. Some actions will likely result in recommendations regarding domestic law provisions, as well as in changes to the Commentary to the OECD Model Tax Convention and the Transfer Pricing Guidelines. Other actions will likely result in changes to the OECD Model Tax Convention. This is for example the case for the introduction of an anti-treaty abuse provision, changes to the definition of permanent establishment, changes to transfer pricing provisions and the introduction of treaty provisions in relation to hybrid mismatch arrangements. Changes to the OECD Model Tax Convention are not directly effective without amendments to bilateral tax treaties. If undertaken on a purely treaty-by-treaty basis, the sheer number of treaties in effect may make such a process very lengthy, the more so where countries embark on comprehensive renegotiations of their bilateral tax treaties. A multilateral instrument to amend bilateral treaties is a promising way forward in this respect.

ACTION 15
Develop a multilateral instrument

Analyse the tax and public international law issues related to the development of a multilateral instrument to enable jurisdictions that wish to do so to implement measures developed in the course of the work on BEPS and amend bilateral tax treaties. On the basis of this analysis, interested Parties will develop a multilateral instrument designed to provide an innovative approach to international tax matters, reflecting the rapidly evolving nature of the global economy and the need to adapt quickly to this evolution.

B. Timing

Addressing BEPS is critical for most countries and must be done in a timely manner, not least to prevent the existing consensus-based framework from unravelling. The pace of the project must be rapid so that concrete actions can be delivered quickly. At the same time, governments also need time to complete the necessary technical work and achieve widespread consensus. Against this background, it is expected that the Action Plan will largely be completed in a two-year period, recognising that some actions will be addressed faster as work has already been advanced, while others might require longer-term work:

- Amongst the actions more likely to be delivered in *12-18 months* are those in the areas of hybrid mismatch arrangements, treaty abuse, the transfer pricing aspects of intangibles, documentation requirements for transfer pricing purposes, a report identifying the issues raised by the digital economy and possible actions to address them, as well as part of the work on harmful tax practices.

- Actions to be delivered *in two years* relate to CFC rules, interest deductibility, preventing the artificial avoidance of PE status, the transfer pricing aspects of intangibles, risks, capital and high-risk transactions, part of the work on harmful tax practices, data collection, mandatory disclosure rules, and dispute resolution.
- Actions that may require *more than two years* include the transfer pricing aspects of financial transactions, part of the work on harmful tax practices and the development of a multilateral instrument to swiftly implement changes to bilateral treaties. Although these actions are considered as key items of the Action Plan, it is recognised that this work will have to be developed in different stages, starting with a thorough analysis of the issues.

Annex A contains tables summarising the different actions and indicating the expected timeline for completing them.

C. Methodology

The BEPS project marks a turning point in the history of international co-operation on taxation. As the current consensus-based framework is at risk, it is critical that a proper methodology be adopted to make sure that the work is inclusive and effective, takes into account the perspective of developing countries and benefits from the input of business and the civil society at large.

(i) An inclusive and effective process: launching the OECD/G20 BEPS Project and involving developing countries

Accomplishing the actions set forth in this Action Plan requires an effective and comprehensive process that involves all relevant stakeholders. To this end, and in order to facilitate greater involvement of major non-OECD economies, the "BEPS Project" will be launched. In light of the strong interest and support expressed on several occasions by the G20, it is proposed that interested G20 countries that are not members of the OECD will be invited to be part of the project as Associates, i.e. on an equal footing with OECD members (including at the level of the subsidiary bodies involved in the work on BEPS), and will be expected to associate themselves with the outcome of the BEPS Project. Other non-members could be invited to participate as Invitees on an ad hoc basis.

Developing countries also face issues related to BEPS, though the issues may manifest differently given the specificities of their legal and administrative frameworks. The UN participates in the tax work of the OECD and will certainly provide useful insights regarding the particular concerns of developing countries. The Task Force on Tax and Development (TFTD) and the OECD Global Relations Programme will provide a useful platform to discuss the specific BEPS concerns in the case of developing countries and explore possible solutions with all stakeholders. Finally, existing mechanisms such as the Global Fora on Tax Treaties, on Transfer Pricing, on VAT and on Transparency and Exchange of Information for Tax Purposes will all be used to involve all countries in the discussions regarding possible technical solutions.

(ii) Efficient process

Political expectations are very high in most countries and the results and impact of the BEPS work must be in line with these political expectations. The BEPS Project will draw on the expertise of the Committee on Fiscal Affairs (CFA) and of its subsidiary bodies. While the practices of these subsidiary bodies are well-adapted to developing consensus on routine work, they require some adaptation to deliver results within the expected timelines. There is thus a need to find ways to accomplish the work quickly while seeking consensus. Each subsidiary body will need to seek new ways to find consensus as quickly as possible. This may involve, for example, setting up focus groups for the actions for which it is responsible. Each focus group could be composed of a relatively small number of delegates, with one country taking the lead and acting as co-ordinator. The focus groups would work actively in between meetings of the relevant subsidiary body, using remote working methods and reducing physical meetings to a minimum, to prepare drafts which would be circulated to and approved by the subsidiary body.

(iii) Consulting with business and civil society

Consultation with non-governmental stakeholders is also key. Business and civil society representatives will be invited to comment on the different proposals developed in the course of the work. The OECD's core relationship with civil society is through the Business and Industry Advisory Committee (BIAC) and the Trade Union Advisory Committee (TUAC) to the OECD. Non-governmental organisations, think tanks, and academia will also be consulted. The OECD's work on the different items of the Action Plan will continue to include a transparent and inclusive consultation process, and a high-level policy dialogue with all interested parties will be organised on an annual basis.

References

G20 (2012), *Leaders Declaration*, Los Cabos, Mexico, www.g20mexico.org/images/stories/docs/g20/conclu/G20_Leaders_Declaration_2012.pdf.

OECD (2013a), *Addressing Base Erosion and Profit Shifting*, OECD Publishing, Paris. doi: 10.1787/9789264192744-en.

OECD (2013b), *Co-operative Compliance: A Framework from Enhanced Relationship to Co-operative Compliance, by the Forum on Tax Administration*, OECD Publishing, Paris. doi: 10.1787/9789264200852-en.

OECD (1998), *Harmful Tax Competition: An Emerging Global Issue*, OECD Publishing, Paris. doi: 10.1787/9789264162945-en.

Annex A

Overview of the actions and timelines

This annex contains summary tables indicating the timeline for the actions included in the Action Plan.

Table A.1. **Summary of the BEPS Action Plan by action**

Action	Description	Expected output	Deadline
1 – **Address the tax challenges of the digital economy**	Identify the main difficulties that the digital economy poses for the application of existing international tax rules and develop detailed options to address these difficulties, taking a holistic approach and considering both direct and indirect taxation. Issues to be examined include, but are not limited to, the ability of a company to have a significant digital presence in the economy of another country without being liable to taxation due to the lack of nexus under current international rules, the attribution of value created from the generation of marketable location-relevant data through the use of digital products and services, the characterisation of income derived from new business models, the application of related source rules, and how to ensure the effective collection of VAT/GST with respect to the cross-border supply of digital goods and services. Such work will require a thorough analysis of the various business models in this sector.	Report identifying issues raised by the digital economy and possible actions to address them	September 2014

Table A.1. **Summary of the BEPS Action Plan by action** *(continued)*

Action	Description	Expected output	Deadline
2 – Neutralise the effects of hybrid mismatch arrangements	*Develop model treaty provisions and recommendations regarding the design of domestic rules to neutralise the effect (e.g. double non-taxation, double deduction, long-term deferral) of hybrid instruments and entities. This may include: (i) changes to the OECD Model Tax Convention to ensure that hybrid instruments and entities (as well as dual resident entities) are not used to obtain the benefits of treaties unduly; (ii) domestic law provisions that prevent exemption or non-recognition for payments that are deductible by the payor; (iii) domestic law provisions that deny a deduction for a payment that is not includible in income by the recipient (and is not subject to taxation under controlled foreign company (CFC) or similar rules); (iv) domestic law provisions that deny a deduction for a payment that is also deductible in another jurisdiction; and (v) where necessary, guidance on co-ordination or tie-breaker rules if more than one country seeks to apply such rules to a transaction or structure. Special attention should be given to the interaction between possible changes to domestic law and the provisions of the OECD Model Tax Convention. This work will be co-ordinated with the work on interest expense deduction limitations, the work on CFC rules, and the work on treaty shopping.*	Changes to the Model Tax Convention	September 2014
		Recommendations regarding the design of domestic rules	September 2014
3 – Strengthen CFC rules	*Develop recommendations regarding the design of controlled foreign company rules. This work will be co-ordinated with other work as necessary.*	Recommendations regarding the design of domestic rules	September 2015

Table A.1. **Summary of the BEPS Action Plan by action** *(continued)*

Action	Description	Expected output	Deadline
4 – Limit base erosion via interest deductions and other financial payments	Develop recommendations regarding best practices in the design of rules to prevent base erosion through the use of interest expense, for example through the use of related-party and third-party debt to achieve excessive interest deductions or to finance the production of exempt or deferred income, and other financial payments that are economically equivalent to interest payments. The work will evaluate the effectiveness of different types of limitations. In connection with and in support of the foregoing work, transfer pricing guidance will also be developed regarding the pricing of related party financial transactions, including financial and performance guarantees, derivatives (including internal derivatives used in intra-bank dealings), and captive and other insurance arrangements. The work will be co-ordinated with the work on hybrids and CFC rules.	Recommendations regarding the design of domestic rules	September 2015
		Changes to the Transfer Pricing Guidelines	December 2015
5 – Counter harmful tax practices more effectively, taking into account transparency and substance	Revamp the work on harmful tax practices with a priority on improving transparency, including compulsory spontaneous exchange on rulings related to preferential regimes, and on requiring substantial activity for any preferential regime. It will take a holistic approach to evaluate preferential tax regimes in the BEPS context. It will engage with non-OECD members on the basis of the existing framework and consider revisions or additions to the existing framework.	Finalise review of member country regimes	September 2014
		Strategy to expand participation to non-OECD members	September 2015
		Revision of existing criteria	December 2015
6 – Prevent treaty abuse	Develop model treaty provisions and recommendations regarding the design of domestic rules to prevent the granting of treaty benefits in inappropriate circumstances. Work will also be done to clarify that tax treaties are not intended to be used to generate double non-taxation and to identify the tax policy considerations that, in general, countries should consider before deciding to enter into a tax treaty with another country. The work will be co-ordinated with the work on hybrids.	Changes to the Model Tax Convention	September 2014
		Recommendations regarding the design of domestic rules	September 2014

Table A.1. **Summary of the BEPS Action Plan by action** *(continued)*

Action	Description	Expected output	Deadline
7 – Prevent the artificial avoidance of PE status	Develop changes to the definition of PE to prevent the artificial avoidance of PE status in relation to BEPS, including through the use of commissionaire arrangements and the specific activity exemptions. Work on these issues will also address related profit attribution issues.	Changes to the Model Tax Convention	September 2015
8 – Assure that transfer pricing outcomes are in line with value creation: intangibles	Develop rules to prevent BEPS by moving intangibles among group members. This will involve: (i) adopting a broad and clearly delineated definition of intangibles; (ii) ensuring that profits associated with the transfer and use of intangibles are appropriately allocated in accordance with (rather than divorced from) value creation; (iii) developing transfer pricing rules or special measures for transfers of hard-to-value intangibles; and (iv) updating the guidance on cost contribution arrangements.	Changes to the Transfer Pricing Guidelines and possibly to the Model Tax Convention	September 2014
		Changes to the Transfer Pricing Guidelines and possibly to the Model Tax Convention	September 2015
9 – Assure that transfer pricing outcomes are in line with value creation: risks and capital	Develop rules to prevent BEPS by transferring risks among, or allocating excessive capital to, group members. This will involve adopting transfer pricing rules or special measures to ensure that inappropriate returns will not accrue to an entity solely because it has contractually assumed risks or has provided capital. The rules to be developed will also require alignment of returns with value creation. This work will be co-ordinated with the work on interest expense deductions and other financial payments.	Changes to the Transfer Pricing Guidelines and possibly to the Model Tax Convention	September 2015
10 – Assure that transfer pricing outcomes are in line with value creation: other high-risk transactions	Develop rules to prevent BEPS by engaging in transactions which would not, or would only very rarely, occur between third parties. This will involve adopting transfer pricing rules or special measures to: (i) clarify the circumstances in which transactions can be recharacterised; (ii) clarify the application of transfer pricing methods, in particular profit splits, in the context of global value chains; and (iii) provide protection against common types of base eroding payments, such as management fees and head office expenses.	Changes to the Transfer Pricing Guidelines and possibly to the Model Tax Convention	September 2015

Table A.1. **Summary of the BEPS Action Plan by action** *(continued)*

Action	Description	Expected output	Deadline
11 – Establish methodologies to collect and analyse data on BEPS and the actions to address it	*Develop recommendations regarding indicators of the scale and economic impact of BEPS and ensure that tools are available to monitor and evaluate the effectiveness and economic impact of the actions taken to address BEPS on an ongoing basis. This will involve developing an economic analysis of the scale and impact of BEPS (including spillover effects across countries) and actions to address it. The work will also involve assessing a range of existing data sources, identifying new types of data that should be collected, and developing methodologies based on both aggregate (e.g. FDI and balance of payments data) and micro-level data (e.g. from financial statements and tax returns), taking into consideration the need to respect taxpayer confidentiality and the administrative costs for tax administrations and businesses.*	Recommendations regarding data to be collected and methodologies to analyse them	September 2015
12 – Require taxpayers to disclose their aggressive tax planning arrangements	*Develop recommendations regarding the design of mandatory disclosure rules for aggressive or abusive transactions, arrangements, or structures, taking into consideration the administrative costs for tax administrations and businesses and drawing on experiences of the increasing number of countries that have such rules. The work will use a modular design allowing for maximum consistency but allowing for country specific needs and risks. One focus will be international tax schemes, where the work will explore using a wide definition of "tax benefit" in order to capture such transactions. The work will be co-ordinated with the work on co-operative compliance. It will also involve designing and putting in place enhanced models of information sharing for international tax schemes between tax administrations.*	Recommendations regarding the design of domestic rules	September 2015

Table A.1. **Summary of the BEPS Action Plan by action** *(continued)*

Action	Description	Expected output	Deadline
13 – Re-examine transfer pricing documentation	Develop rules regarding transfer pricing documentation to enhance transparency for tax administration, taking into consideration the compliance costs for business. The rules to be developed will include a requirement that MNE's provide all relevant governments with needed information on their global allocation of the income, economic activity and taxes paid among countries according to a common template.	Changes to Transfer Pricing Guidelines and Recommendations regarding the design of domestic rules	September 2014
14 – Make dispute resolution mechanisms more effective	Develop solutions to address obstacles that prevent countries from solving treaty-related disputes under MAP, including the absence of arbitration provisions in most treaties and the fact that access to MAP and arbitration may be denied in certain cases.	Changes to the Model Tax Convention	September 2015
15 – Develop a multilateral instrument	Analyse the tax and public international law issues related to the development of a multilateral instrument to enable jurisdictions that wish to do so to implement measures developed in the course of the work on BEPS and amend bilateral tax treaties. On the basis of this analysis, interested Parties will develop a multilateral instrument designed to provide an innovative approach to international tax matters, reflecting the rapidly evolving nature of the global economy and the need to adapt quickly to this evolution.	Report identifying relevant public international law and tax issues	September 2014
		Develop a multilateral instrument	December 2015

Table A.2. **Summary of the BEPS Action Plan by timeline**

	BY SEPTEMBER 2014	
Action	Description	Expected Output
Address the tax challenges of the digital economy	Identify the main difficulties that the digital economy poses for the application of existing international tax rules and develop detailed options to address these difficulties, taking a holistic approach and considering both direct and indirect taxation. Issues to be examined include, but are not limited to, the ability of a company to have a significant digital presence in the economy of another country without being liable to taxation due to the lack of nexus under current international rules, the attribution of value created from the generation of marketable location-relevant data through the use of digital products and services, the characterisation of income derived from new business models, the application of related source rules, and how to ensure the effective collection of VAT/GST with respect to the cross-border supply of digital goods and services. Such work will require a thorough analysis of the various business models in this sector.	Report identifying issues raised by the digital economy and possible actions to address them
Neutralise the effects of hybrid mismatch arrangements	Develop model treaty provisions and recommendations regarding the design of domestic rules to neutralise the effect (e.g. double non-taxation, double deduction, long-term deferral) of hybrid instruments and entities. This may include: (i) changes to the OECD Model Tax Convention to ensure that hybrid instruments and entities (as well as dual resident entities) are not used to obtain the benefits of treaties unduly; (ii) domestic law provisions that prevent exemption or non-recognition for payments that are deductible by the payor; (iii) domestic law provisions that deny a deduction for a payment that is not includible in income by the recipient (and is not subject to taxation under controlled foreign company (CFC) or similar rules); (iv) domestic law provisions that deny a deduction for a payment that is also deductible in another jurisdiction; and (v) where necessary, guidance on co-ordination or tie-breaker rules if more than one country seeks to apply such rules to a transaction or structure. Special attention should be given to the interaction between possible changes to domestic law and the provisions of the OECD Model Tax Convention. This work will be co-ordinated with the work on interest expense deduction limitations, the work on CFC rules, and the work on treaty shopping.	Changes to the Model Tax Convention Recommendations regarding the design of domestic rules

Table A.2. **Summary of the BEPS Action Plan by timeline** *(continued)*

Action	BY SEPTEMBER 2014	
	Description	Expected Output
Counter harmful tax practices more effectively, taking into account transparency and substance – *phase 1*	*Revamp the work on harmful tax practices with a priority on improving transparency, including compulsory spontaneous exchange on rulings related to preferential regimes, and on requiring substantial activity for any preferential regime. It will take a holistic approach to evaluate preferential tax regimes in the BEPS context. It will engage with non-OECD members on the basis of the existing framework and consider revisions or additions to the existing framework.*	Finalise review of member country regimes
Prevent treaty abuse	*Develop model treaty provisions and recommendations regarding the design of domestic rules to prevent the granting of treaty benefits in inappropriate circumstances. Work will also be done to clarify that tax treaties are not intended to be used to generate double non-taxation and to identify the tax policy considerations that, in general, countries should consider before deciding to enter into a tax treaty with another country. The work will be co-ordinated with the work on hybrids.*	Changes to the Model Tax Convention Recommendations regarding the design of domestic rules
Assure that transfer pricing outcomes are in line with value creation: intangibles – *phase 1*	*Develop rules to prevent BEPS by moving intangibles among group members. This will involve: (i) adopting a broad and clearly delineated definition of intangibles; (ii) ensuring that profits associated with the transfer and use of intangibles are appropriately allocated in accordance with (rather than divorced from) value creation; …*	Changes to the Transfer Pricing Guidelines and possibly to the Model Tax Convention
Re-examine transfer pricing documentation	*Develop rules regarding transfer pricing documentation to enhance transparency for tax administration, taking into consideration the compliance costs for business. The rules to be developed will include a requirement that MNE's provide all relevant governments with needed information on their global allocation of the income, economic activity and taxes paid among countries according to a common template.*	Changes to Transfer Pricing Guidelines and Recommendations regarding the design of domestic rules

Table A.2. **Summary of the BEPS Action Plan by timeline** *(continued)*

	BY SEPTEMBER 2014	
Action	Description	Expected Output
Develop a multilateral instrument – phase 1	*Analyse the tax and public international law issues related to the development of a multilateral instrument to enable jurisdictions that wish to do so to implement measures developed in the course of the work on BEPS and amend bilateral tax treaties. On the basis of this analysis, interested Parties will develop a multilateral instrument designed to provide an innovative approach to international tax matters, reflecting the rapidly evolving nature of the global economy and the need to adapt quickly to this evolution.*	Report identifying relevant public international law and tax issues

	BY SEPTEMBER 2015	
Action	Description	Expected Output
Strengthen CFC rules	*Develop recommendations regarding the design of controlled foreign company rules. This work will be co-ordinated with other work as necessary.*	Recommendations regarding the design of domestic rules
Limit base erosion via interest deductions and other financial payments	*Develop recommendations regarding best practices in the design of rules to prevent base erosion through the use of interest expense, for example through the use of related-party and third-party debt to achieve excessive interest deductions or to finance the production of exempt or deferred income, and other financial payments that are economically equivalent to interest payments. The work will evaluate the effectiveness of different types of limitations. In connection with and in support of the foregoing work, transfer pricing guidance will also be developed regarding the pricing of related party financial transactions, including financial and performance guarantees, derivatives (including internal derivatives used in intra-bank dealings), and captive and other insurance arrangements. The work will be co-ordinated with the work on hybrids and CFC rules.*	Recommendations regarding the design of domestic rules

Table A.2. **Summary of the BEPS Action Plan by timeline** *(continued)*

Action	BY SEPTEMBER 2015 Description	Expected Output
Counter harmful tax practices more effectively, taking into account transparency and substance – phase 2	*Revamp the work on harmful tax practices with a priority on improving transparency, including compulsory spontaneous exchange on rulings related to preferential regimes, and on requiring substantial activity for any preferential regime. It will take a holistic approach to evaluate preferential tax regimes in the BEPS context. It will engage with non-OECD members on the basis of the existing framework and consider revisions or additions to the existing framework.*	Strategy to expand participation to non-OECD members
Prevent the artificial avoidance of PE status	*Develop changes to the definition of PE to prevent the artificial avoidance of PE status in relation to BEPS, including through the use of commissionaire arrangements and the specific activity exemptions. Work on these issues will also address related profit attribution issues.*	Changes to the Model Tax Convention
Assure that transfer pricing outcomes are in line with value creation: intangibles – phase 2	*Develop rules to prevent BEPS by moving intangibles among group members. This will involve: … (iii) developing transfer pricing rules or special measures for transfers of hard-to-value intangibles; and (iv) updating the guidance on cost contribution arrangements.*	Changes to the Transfer Pricing Guidelines and possibly to the Model Tax Convention
Assure that transfer pricing outcomes are in line with value creation: risks and capital	*Develop rules to prevent BEPS by transferring risks among, or allocating excessive capital to, group members. This will involve adopting transfer pricing rules or special measures to ensure that inappropriate returns will not accrue to an entity solely because it has contractually assumed risks or has provided capital. The rules to be developed will also require alignment of returns with value creation. This work will be co-ordinated with the work on interest expense deductions and other financial payments.*	Changes to the Transfer Pricing Guidelines and possibly to the Model Tax Convention
Assure that transfer pricing outcomes are in line with value creation/other high-risk transactions	*Develop rules to prevent BEPS by engaging in transactions which would not, or would only very rarely, occur between third parties. This will involve adopting transfer pricing rules or special measures to: (i) clarify the circumstances in which transactions can be recharacterised; (ii) clarify the application of transfer pricing methods, in particular profit splits, in the context of global value chains; and (iii) provide protection against common types of base eroding payments, such as management fees and head office expenses.*	Changes to the Transfer Pricing Guidelines and possibly to the Model Tax Convention

Table A.2. **Summary of the BEPS Action Plan by timeline** *(continued)*

Action	BY SEPTEMBER 2015	
	Description	Expected Output
Establish methodologies to collect and analyse data on beps and the actions to address it	*Develop recommendations regarding indicators of the scale and economic impact of BEPS and ensure that tools are available to monitor and evaluate the effectiveness and economic impact of the actions taken to address BEPS on an ongoing basis. This will involve developing an economic analysis of the scale and impact of BEPS (including spillover effects across countries) and actions to address it. The work will also involve assessing a range of existing data sources, identifying new types of data that should be collected, and developing methodologies based on both aggregate (e.g. FDI and balance of payments data) and micro-level data (e.g. from financial statements and tax returns), taking into consideration the need to respect taxpayer confidentiality and the administrative costs for tax administrations and businesses.*	Recommendations regarding data to be collected and methodologies to analyse them
Require taxpayers to disclose their aggressive tax planning arrangements	*Develop recommendations regarding the design of mandatory disclosure rules for aggressive or abusive transactions, arrangements, or structures, taking into consideration the administrative costs for tax administrations and businesses and drawing on experiences of the increasing number of countries that have such rules. The work will use a modular design allowing for maximum consistency but allowing for country specific needs and risks. One focus will be international tax schemes, where the work will explore using a wide definition of "tax benefit" in order to capture such transactions. The work will be co-ordinated with the work on co-operative compliance. It will also involve designing and putting in place enhanced models of information sharing for international tax schemes between tax administrations.*	Recommendations regarding the design of domestic rules
Make dispute resolution mechanisms more effective	*Develop solutions to address obstacles that prevent countries from solving treaty-related disputes under MAP, including the absence of arbitration provisions in most treaties and the fact that access to MAP and arbitration may be denied in certain cases.*	Changes to the Model Tax Convention

Table A.2. **Summary of the BEPS Action Plan by timeline** *(continued)*

Action	Description	Expected Output
	BY DECEMBER 2015	
Limit base erosion via interest deductions – phase 2	*Develop recommendations regarding best practices in the design of rules to prevent base erosion through the use of interest expense, for example through the use of related-party and third-party debt to achieve excessive interest deductions or to finance the production of exempt or deferred income, and other financial payments that are economically equivalent to interest payments. The work will evaluate the effectiveness of different types of limitations. In connection with and in support of the foregoing work, transfer pricing guidance will also be developed regarding the pricing of related party financial transactions, including financial and performance guarantees, derivatives (including internal derivatives used in intra-bank dealings), and captive and other insurance arrangements. The work will be co-ordinated with the work on hybrids and CFC rules.*	Changes to the Transfer Pricing Guidelines
Counter harmful tax practices more effectively, taking into account transparency and substance – phase 3	*Revamp the work on harmful tax practices with a priority on improving transparency, including compulsory spontaneous exchange on rulings related to preferential regimes, and on requiring substantial activity for any preferential regime. It will take a holistic approach to evaluate preferential tax regimes in the BEPS context. It will engage with non-OECD members on the basis of the existing framework and consider revisions or additions to the existing framework.*	Revision of existing criteria to identify harmful tax practices
Develop a multilateral instrument – phase 2	*Analyse the tax and public international law issues related to the development of a multilateral instrument to enable jurisdictions that wish to do so to implement measures developed in the course of the work on BEPS and amend bilateral tax treaties. On the basis of this analysis, interested Parties will develop a multilateral instrument designed to provide an innovative approach to international tax matters, reflecting the rapidly evolving nature of the global economy and the need to adapt quickly to this evolution.*	Multilateral instrument

ORGANISATION FOR ECONOMIC CO-OPERATION AND DEVELOPMENT

The OECD is a unique forum where governments work together to address the economic, social and environmental challenges of globalisation. The OECD is also at the forefront of efforts to understand and to help governments respond to new developments and concerns, such as corporate governance, the information economy and the challenges of an ageing population. The Organisation provides a setting where governments can compare policy experiences, seek answers to common problems, identify good practice and work to co-ordinate domestic and international policies.

The OECD member countries are: Australia, Austria, Belgium, Canada, Chile, the Czech Republic, Denmark, Estonia, Finland, France, Germany, Greece, Hungary, Iceland, Ireland, Israel, Italy, Japan, Korea, Luxembourg, Mexico, the Netherlands, New Zealand, Norway, Poland, Portugal, the Slovak Republic, Slovenia, Spain, Sweden, Switzerland, Turkey, the United Kingdom and the United States. The European Union takes part in the work of the OECD.

OECD Publishing disseminates widely the results of the Organisation's statistics gathering and research on economic, social and environmental issues, as well as the conventions, guidelines and standards agreed by its members.

Notes

Notes

Notes

Lightning Source UK Ltd.
Milton Keynes UK
UKOW07f1147251114

242147UK00001B/2/P